WORRY LESS

Honor Head

W

FRANKLIN WATTS

LONDON • SYDNEY

Published in paperback in Great Britain in 2020
by The Watts Publishing Group
© The Watts Publishing Group 2020

Managing editor: Victoria Brooker
Design: Sophie Burdess

Image credits: Shutterstock – all images Good Studio apart
from Dooder 29tc, Macrovector 29t.

Every attempt has been made to clear copyright.
Should there be any inadvertent omission
please apply to the publisher for rectification.

ISBN: ISBN 9781445170626 (hbk)
ISBN: 9781445170633 (pbk)

Printed in China

Franklin Watts
An imprint of
Hachette Children's Group
Part of the Watts Publishing Group
Carmelite House
50 Victoria Embankment
London EC4Y 0DZ
An Hachette UK Company
www.hachette.co.uk
www.franklinwatts.co.uk

CONTENTS

WHAT IS WORRY?

Worry is when you feel anxious or concerned about things.
Worries make you feel scared and stop you enjoying
life and having fun.

SOME WORRIES ARE PERSONAL ...

What if Mum and
Dad split up?

Why did I argue with
my best friend?

What if no one likes me?

What should
I wear?

Will I fit in?

Will I make
the sports team?

What if I hate
my new school?

Will I pass
my exams?

I have too much
homework.

SOME WORRIES ARE WORLDWIDE ...

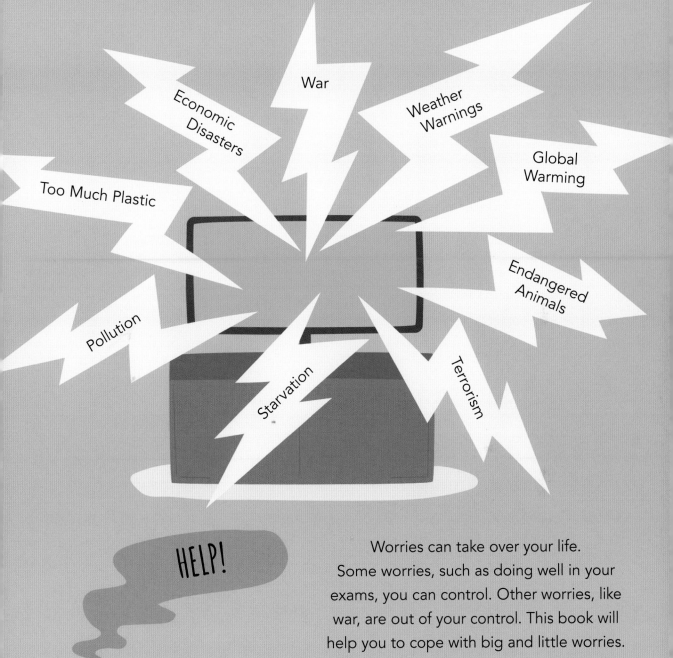

War

Economic Disasters

Weather Warnings

Global Warming

Too Much Plastic

Endangered Animals

Pollution

Starvation

Terrorism

HELP!

Worries can take over your life. Some worries, such as doing well in your exams, you can control. Other worries, like war, are out of your control. This book will help you to cope with big and little worries.

1. CONTROL YOUR WORRY

Worry, worry, worry… sometimes it might feel as if your head is going to explode. Stop!

Write down your worries – it can help to get them out of your head.

Try and use as few words as possible to describe the worry. This helps to make it seem smaller.

Think about what you can do to stop the worry. For example, if you are worried about an exam, make sure you have a revision schedule.

Replace the worry with positive thinking. If you fail the exam is it really the end of the world? You can always try again.

Ask yourself what is the worst that can happen. So 'what if I fail my exam' becomes 'I am going to do my best in this exam'.

Don't feed your worry by thinking about it all the time.

Do things you
enjoy – have fun.
This will help to
take your mind
off the worry.

Talk to someone –
an adult you trust,
a friend or phone
a helpline. Often
when we share a
worry, it seems
less scary.

Sometimes when you're not thinking
about it, the worry vanishes!

2. NEW SCHOOL CHALLENGE

New building, new friends, new teachers, new classes ...
here's how to handle any new school worries.

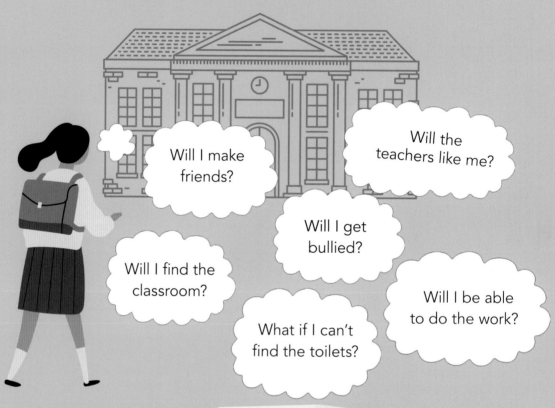

- Talk about your worries with parents or carers.

- See if the school offers an open evening or day when you can look around and meet the teachers.

- Make a checklist ... this puts you in control.

GET READY THE NIGHT BEFORE:

- Hang your uniform out.
- Pack your school bag.
- Check transport times or route if walking.
- Arrange to meet up with some old friends after school. It will give you something positive to look forward to.
- Get a good night's sleep.

FIRST DAY:

- Get up early enough to eat breakfast without rushing.

- Take a few deep breaths, grab your bag, go!

- Plan to get to school a little earlier to give yourself time to find the cloakrooms, the toilets and your first classroom.

- It is okay to feel a little worried. Probably everyone else is, too.

- Smile!

- Be friendly with your new classmates. These are all potential new friends.

- Be respectful and concentrate in class – first impressions count!

- By the end of the week you'll wonder what you ever worried about!

3. HANDLE PEER PRESSURE

People your own age or your peers can influence
how you think and behave, and you do the same to them.

Come with us.
We're not going to
school today.

*If I don't they
won't be friends
with me.*

If you climb
to the top, you
can be part of
our group.

*It's dangerous,
but I want to be
part of the group.*

*I don't want to
be mean, but if
I don't they will
turn on me.*

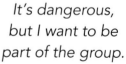

Being put under this kind of pressure can cause worries
about losing friends and not being accepted.
It can be tough, but you have to do what you think is right.

SCENARIO 1:

I don't want to
get into trouble.

*Who needs
friends like
that anyway!*

SCENARIO 2:

*It's a stupid
thing to do.*

Mum's
expecting me
home.

SCENARIO 3:

*It's wrong to
hurt people
for fun.*

I think
that's mean.

Choose friends who are kind,
caring and respect your wishes.
And don't worry about being
friends with people who
are not worth it.

4. FIGHT SOCIAL MEDIA ANXIETY

Social media is great, but it can cause lots of worries.

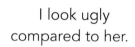

I look ugly compared to her.

Why is no one messaging me?

I missed a text ... Oh no! FOMO!

Why wasn't I invited to that party?

Only 3 likes ... what's wrong with my picture?

It's easy to worry about your online presence, how you appear to everyone and how your life compares to theirs.

To help you feel less anxious about social media
you need to build up your self-esteem.

Be proud of
who you are.

Remember you are
unique and have
your own style.

Spend more time
face-to-face having
fun with real friends.

It is normal to feel hurt and
angry if you are left out of social
media stuff, but try to move on.

List all the things
you like about
yourself.

Try shutting down
social media for even
just an hour a day.

List all the things
you are good at.

Learn new things,
try a new hobby
or join a club.

5. DEAL WITH BULLYING

Here are some ways to cope with bullies, on and offline.

WHAT IS CYBERBULLYING?

- Being blocked for no reason.
- Being made fun of in a way that is hurtful and unkind.
- Being sent nasty messages or threats.
- Embarrassing photos posted online without your permission.

- Block people who abuse or embarrass you.
- Switch off – the cyberbullies will soon get bored.
- Report nasty messages to an adult or the police.
- Don't talk back – this encourages bullies.
- Don't like or share anything that is mean or nasty.

STAND UP TO BULLYING!

It is your right to be safe at home, at school and in public places.

It is not your fault you are being bullied.

You are not weak and the bully is not strong.

Look a bully in the eye, stand tall and tell the bully to back off in a calm but firm voice.

Remember, bullies are cowards!

Report all bullying.

6. UNDERSTAND PUBERTY

Between the ages of about 8 and 14 your body begins to change as you start to go through puberty.

ZITS

SWEATING

HAIR GROWING

GROWTH SPURTS

DEEPER VOICE

MOOD SWINGS

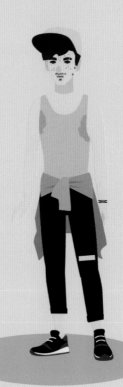

All this is normal. Changes can be scary, but it is nothing to worry about.

It's not just your body that's changing.
Your feelings can seem like an emotional roller coaster ...

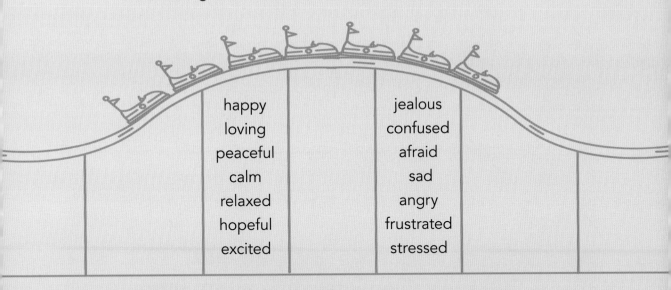

happy	jealous
loving	confused
peaceful	afraid
calm	sad
relaxed	angry
hopeful	frustrated
excited	stressed

YOU CAN COPE WITH PUBERTY!

Eat plenty
of fresh
fruit
and veg.

Worried?
Talk to
someone
about it.

Drink lots
of water.

Get a good
night's sleep ...
your brain
and body
need it.

Exercise –
it will release
feel-good
hormones into
your body.

Practise
relaxation
techniques
(see page 26).

STAY POSITIVE, PUBERTY WILL PASS.

It is an exciting journey to the next stage of your life.

7. DEAL WITH ANXIETY OVER WORLD ISSUES

There is a lot of challenging stuff going on in the world
that could make you feel scared and angry.

ANIMAL EXTINCTION

TORTURE

FLOODS

HOMELESSNESS

CLIMATE CHANGE

BOMBS

FAMINE

NEWS

REFUGEES

WAR

POVERTY

These are all issues that are out of your control.
That doesn't mean you have to ignore them.
Instead of worrying, think of ways you can help.

HELP TO SAVE THE WORLD!

Okay, not quite saving the world, but channel the energy you use worrying into doing something positive.

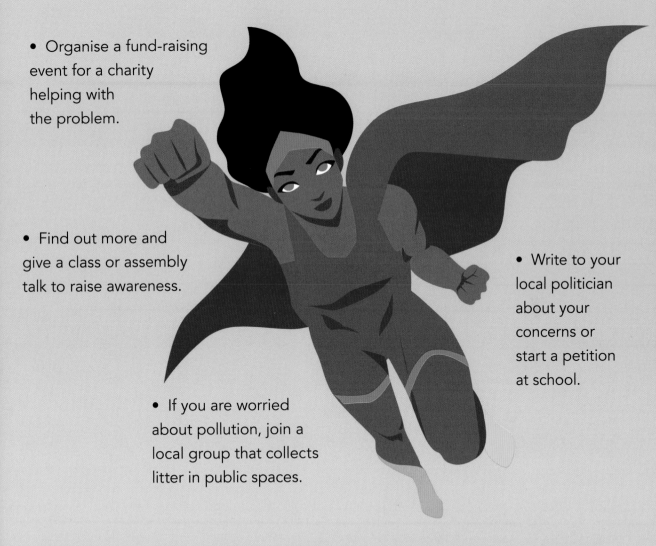

• Organise a fund-raising event for a charity helping with the problem.

• Find out more and give a class or assembly talk to raise awareness.

• Write to your local politician about your concerns or start a petition at school.

• If you are worried about pollution, join a local group that collects litter in public spaces.

NOT ONLY WILL YOU BE DOING SOMETHING TO HELP YOU STOP WORRYING, YOU CAN FEEL PROUD THAT YOU ARE HELPING.

8. TACKLE NIGHT-TIME WORRIES

It's dark. You are trying to sleep. Your head is filled with worries.
You toss and turn and the worries seem to get bigger and darker …

SOCIAL MEDIA

GLOBAL WARMING

EXAMS

SPOTS

FRIENDS

FAMILY

BAD HAIR

MATHS TEST

Most people will have night-time worries at some time …
it is quite normal. But getting a good night's sleep is really important.
While you sleep your brain helps to sort out all your worries.
So help your brain to get some sleep …

BEFORE BED:

Use lavender smellies at bedtime. Lavender is good for helping the brain and body to relax.

Avoid screens about an hour before bed. Blue light from the screen stops your brain slowing down for sleep.

Write down your worries and say you will think about them in the morning. Chances are they will be gone by then or won't look so bad in daylight.

Have a warm shower or bath.

Have a warm milky drink or camomile tea.

Sleep well

9. CONTROL PANIC ATTACKS

Panic attacks are very scary. They can happen when worries grow.

SCARED

FEAR

AM I GOING CRAZY?

FEELING FAINT

SICK

DIZZY

FAST HEART

CAN'T BREATHE

SWEATING

CHOKING FEELING

SHAKING

SOMETHING AWFUL WILL HAPPEN

Panic attacks are frightening, but they are not dangerous.

WHAT TO DO...

 Remember this is temporary and it will pass quickly. Panic attacks last about 10 minutes.

 Breathe slowly and deeply.

 If you are alone, phone someone you trust and talk to them until you feel better.

 Look at photos on your phone to take your mind off the panic.

 Focus on what is going on around you. What can you hear, see, smell?

After the attack, think about what could have triggered it. What are you feeling anxious about? Talk about your worries or write them down to get them out of your head.

 If you have panic attacks a lot, speak to your doctor or a specialist.

23

10. LET GO OF WORRIES

Instead of letting worries fill your head, focus on really important things.

GOALS

Write down your goals. Think about how you can achieve them.

Think about your goals. You can make plans for next week or for when you leave school.

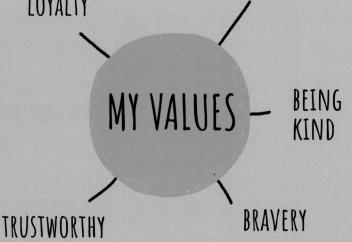

HELPING PEOPLE

LOYALTY

If you are worrying about a situation and what to do, think about your values. It could help you make a decision.

MY VALUES

BEING KIND

TRUSTWORTHY

BRAVERY

Learning a new sport or hobby, or trying something new, will help you forget your worries. And you'll meet new people and feel a sense of achievement.

LEARN NEW STUFF

Go online, contact your local gym or look for clubs to see what new things you can try.

I'm sorry!

Next time!

I FORGIVE ME!

I can take it again.

Worrying about what you said wrong, did wrong or should have done that you didn't do is pointless. Everyone makes mistakes, fails and messes up. Learn from your mistakes, forgive yourself and move on.

11. RELAX

Instead of letting worries fill your head, focus on really important things.

AND ... BREATHE!

Do this once a day or any time you feel worried.

- Lie down.
- Close your eyes.
- Take a deep breath in through your nose.
- Feel your tummy fill with air like a balloon.
- Breathe out through your mouth.
- Feel your tummy go down.
- Breathe slowly ... count to three on the in breath and out breath.
- Repeat 5 to 10 times.

RELAX YOUR MUSCLES

- Sit or lie down.
- Close your eyes.
- Starting with your toes, tense your muscles ... toes ... legs ... stomach ... chest ...hands ... arms ... back ... neck ...jaw ... face ...
- Then relax them all one by one.
- Do this once a day and when you feel stressed.

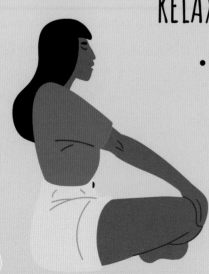

TRY YOGA

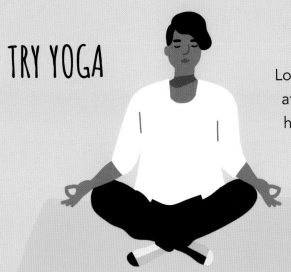

Look out for classes at your local gym, hall or community centre.

A SAFE SPACE

Find a safe, happy place in your head that you can go to when you feel anxious or stressed.

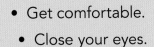

- Get comfortable.
- Close your eyes.
  - Think of a place where you are really happy.
  - Picture it in your mind in as much detail as possible. What can you see, feel, hear and touch? See yourself there safe and smiling.
  - Go there when you feel really anxious or worried to calm down before carrying on.

12. THINK POSITIVE

Developing positive thinking techniques
can help you banish worries and anxiety.

VISUALISE

Think about a situation that worries you.
Then visualise yourself doing that thing brilliantly.
Think about how good you feel.
See yourself smiling and happy.

BE POSITIVE

I don't deserve
to be happy.

Maths is too
hard for me.

I have a right to be safe
and happy like
everyone else.

I will I keep trying.
Perhaps my teacher
can help.

Stamp out negative speak!
Turn everything negative you think
or say to yourself into a positive.

MAKE AN ACHIEVEMENTS BOX

This is great for when you feel sad or negative ... it will remind you of all the good stuff that has happened to you, how much you have achieved and what you have to be grateful for. Take it out and have a look when you feel anxious or worried.

BE OPTIMISTIC

Worriers expect the worst to happen – they will fail the exam, not make the football team, lose their friends and not get any likes online. Sometimes life is unfair, things go wrong and bad things happen. But always think that the best will happen and more often than not it will. And if it doesn't, your optimistic and positive outlook will help you to cope.

WHERE TO GET HELP

If you feel that worry is taking over your life or you have lots of panic attacks or anxiety, you must speak to someone. Try and talk to your carers, a trusted adult, a teacher or your friends about how you feel. If there is no one you want to talk to, there are loads of places online that can help you. Chat rooms and forums are great for talking to people who feel the same way as you do and may have had similar experiences. However, never share personal details with anyone, no matter how genuine they seem. Never meet up with strangers.

Telephone helplines are places where you can talk to someone who is specially trained to understand what you are going through. They won't judge you or make you do anything you don't want to do. You don't have to be embarrassed or ashamed or silly about what you tell them. They will be understanding, kind and supportive.

www.childline.org.uk/info-advice/yourfeelings/mental-health
Message or call the 24 hour helpline
for advice or someone who'll just listen.
The helpline is 0800 1111

https://papyrus-uk.org
A place to go if you have bad thoughts
about harming yourself or suicide.
HopelineUK 0800 068 41 41

www.samaritans.org
A place where anyone can go for
advice and comfort.
The helpline is 08457 90 90 90

www.sane.org/get-help
Help and support for anyone affected
by mental and emotional issues.
The helpline is 0300 304 7000

www.supportline.org.uk
A charity giving emotional
support to young people.
The helpline is 01708 765200

kidshealth.org/en/kids/feeling
Advice on managing emotions.

www.youngminds.org.uk
Advice for young people
experiencing bullying, stress
and mental or emotional anxieties.

**www.brainline.org/content/2009/05/
who-me-self-esteem-for-people-with disabilities.html**
How to boost self-esteem
regardless of disabilities.

SHOUT!
A text only 24/7 helpline for anyone suffering from
emotional and mental issues or going through a crisis.
Text 85258 and a trained volunteer will be there to help.

Or settle down with a book ...

The Unworry Book
by Alice James, Usborne, 2019

Create Your Own Happy
by Penny Alexander and Becky Goddard-Hill,
Collins 2018

GLOSSARY

anxious feeling worried or nervous about how something is going to turn out
concentrate focus on what you are doing
extinction when something, such as animal or plant, is dying out
FOMO acronym for 'Fear Of Missing Out'
hormone chemical substance in your body that keeps it working properly
impressions the feelings or ideas you get about something
peers people of your own age, such as friends and classmates
positive thinking believing the best about a situation
pressure feeling a person or situation is forcing you to achieve something quickly or well
respectful in a way that takes other people's feelings into consideration
values the rules you live by, such as being honest and kind

INDEX